3/30/73

Mom -

Hope your
birthday is
great - wish
I was there (or
you were here) -

Love!
Joanne

CATS

CATS

EDITED BY HANNS REICH

TEXT BY EUGEN SKASA-WEISS

HILL AND WANG · NEW YORK
A DIVISION OF FARRAR, STRAUS AND GIROUX, INC.

Copyright © 1965 by Hanns Reich Verlag,
a division of McGraw-Hill Book Company GmbH, Düsseldorf
All rights reserved
Published in the United States of America by
Hill and Wang, a division of Farrar, Straus and Giroux, Inc.
ISBN: 0-8090-2025-4
Library of Congress catalog card number: 62-15220
Published simultaneously in Canada by
Doubleday Canada Ltd., Toronto
Production Office: Rudolf P. Gorbach, Munich
Manufactured by Arts Graphiques Héliographia S. A., Lausanne
Printed in Switzerland

Everywhere in the world cats are full of charm and originality. To a confirmed cat lover this will come as no revelation. But perhaps it will surprise the other viewers of this book who may be really meeting cats for the first time here. Maybe this book shall win new friends for cats. Who doesn't admire the beautiful once he becomes aware of it?

Violets are not shrinking, doves are not particularly peaceful, and cats, contrary to a common notion, are neither false nor cruel.

Nonetheless, these graceful and decidedly temperamental animals maintain a certain aloofness in their relations with humans, especially since, from a cat's point of view, most people lead lives that are much too strenuous. Also, subtly discreet and reserved, cats distrust the world man has put together – a world as different as can be from the easygoing world of the cat.

Loud-mouths and cats never get along. But every cat with a sense of humor has fun testing timid souls. You often see a cat climb up an unwilling lap. Since cats have a kind of secret radar which tells them who likes them and who does not, I am never sure whether they are trying to convert anti-cat humans, or merely deriving paradoxical pleasure in ruffling tensed, hostile people, who must sit and endure it.

At any rate, the most passionate devotees are the converts – those who one day are suddenly filled with love for cats. Many a man who has tossed beer cans at a howling alley cat changes his mind about cats as he watches a kitten repeatedly leap at a moth. He soon discovers joy and well-being in a tomcat's purr.

If you shudder to find a little bird's feather on the whisker of a kitten, you will never feel at home in the fundamentally simple world of the cat. You will never appreciate a kitten's heavenly beauty or innocence.

Cats cause sharp differences of opinion. You may not like one because it is too quiet or too stubborn, but someone else may like it for just those reasons. Very few people fail to react to the blinking of a cat's eyes. The shimmer of sunlight on the crackling fur of a cat gives some people goose pimples. (Isn't there an Oriental legend which says that human beings were rats in a previous incarnation?)

If there were no cats, no one would be able to invent them. For these hybrid creatures, a cross between animal and gnome, with their sleek lines, ceremonial airs, and unexpected leaps, are by no mean simple. An artist who has never watched a cat asleep or at play could not recreate out of his imagination such a combination of polished elegance and potential fury. The cat is the animal to which poets, painters, witches, and children bow in fascinated admiration.

It speaks volumes for the early peoples of ancient Egypt that the freedom-loving cat allowed itself to be domesticated by them. The Egyptians in turn were so grateful that they honored their trusting and amiable pet as a god.

No one can get very far in analyzing cats because each cat is an individual that has to be thoroughly studied and each always manages to retain a little secret of its own. Most cats are able, in the most charming way, to demolish the cat stereotype.

Only persons whose experience with cats is brief and limited can make categorical assertions about their habits and preferences. We can say that most cats love to play games and beg for things. For hygienic reasons they like to chew grass. But differences in their tastes begin with food. Some definitely prefer green beans to raw liver; many turn up their noses at cow's milk. Some catch mice only with an atavistic hauteur and then drop them like empty purses so they can proceed to nibble on raw potato peels. I know cats who love to smell roses. There are artistically flawless tight-rope walking cats who never in their life have overturned a vase or pushed a plate from a table. But there are others who, with a wild meow, tumble and fall like clowns into a bowl of flour or the bathtub. Everything is conceivable with cats. There are talkative and taciturn felines, tight-lipped stoics, and loud howlers who react in some way to everything and feel obliged to comment at length on every event. I knew a male cat who had it in for electric razors as the parts were being assembled; his mate, whom he incessantly raged at, took offence only when the buzzing razor came near a human chin.

One thing – and a most annoying thing – is probably common to all cats: their habit of pausing stock-still on the threshold. Watch a cat who has pleaded passionately from behind a closed door to be let in. Once the door is opened, does she enter? No, her legs stiffen, she hoists her tail, and puts her engine into low gear. She has to give the matter a great deal of thought.

Growing impatient, I call to the cat. She looks up skeptically, tentatively pushes her head a little forward, and studies me. "Come in, kitty!" Disgusting, thinks kitty. She's in a bad mood today. She withdraws in dignity, lowers her upturned tail, and sits on it. Then she rises hesitantly, stretches, moves her head slightly forward....

I begin to boil. In my impatience, I press against the door. The cat pulls back her head; she refuses to enter a trap. She casts several absent-minded glances over the floor. Again she pauses on the threshold, transfixed. She cannot refrain from pausing first on the threshold to rub against the doorpost and shut her eyes. But I in my impatience am definitely not in the mood for this self-indulgent pleasure. It is a moment of maximum danger between me and the cat. I raise my hand to shut the door again. Then occurs what the cat has instinctively feared: her tail gets jammed. She howls, hisses, and quickly hides. Her skepticism has been confirmed. Not with impunity can a cat hurry through an open door. It is a gamble and will always be a gamble. Man is false.

Suppose you have two cats. One is in the room while the other is outside the door meowing to be let in. The cat inside wants to join its playmate in the hall. You open the door to bring them together. What happens? The hall cat comes in and the other cat passes right by. If you shut the door, the game repeats itself. The cats walk past each other like figures on a toy clock.

When they want to, cats catch mice with lightning speed. But when you want them to show speed, they indulge in such studied contemplation that you would not tolerate even in the loveliest woman in the world. A beautiful woman who keeps you on tenterhooks arouses your ire. But a person who knows and loves cats suppresses the angry look.

Of course, this pause on the threshold takes place only if the cat has urgently pleaded to be let in or out. If a cat is not supposed to go out, it manages to slip through the doorway quicker than a mouse. You barely catch sight of it as it whisks through the smallest opening.

Cats differ widely in character and temperament in the way they greet their masters. Some of them, after a long separation, may take virtually no notice of their master on his return. They are content to observe him silently. Others celebrate the event with frantic purring and dancing, rubbing their little pink or black nose against the long-absent chin. Then, too, the same cat may decide to vary its greeting, explosive on one occasion, disdainful on another. But most cats do remember to give some kind of a genuine welcome with their heads as they plunge into the food parcel set before them. Those of you who have Siamese cats know how fearfully they have sobbed and wailed on being left behind. But on your return, what happens? They greet you reproachfully, sulkily, nonchalantly, or with a rather frivolous gaiety. And you love them all the more for it. Aristocratic cats, attached to one person for years (they would not dream of getting close to more than two persons in their entire lifetime) go to pieces if they have to leave their master and put up with someone else.

The ties between cats and human beings, when there is affection on both sides, are not material ones. When we are in a bad mood, cats behave with contempt toward us and their food plates as well. When cat owners fail to behave like ladies and gentlemen, their cats never weary of reminding them that the deeper ties between them must be woven of subtle, tender, considerate, and eccentric threads. Women often criticize men for their harsh tone, their appalling lack of attention and tenderness. A Siamese behaves the same way toward a human who does not greet it properly or brushes it aside. On occasion, this protest takes the form of an ear-splitting yowling that goes on without a let-up. My Siamese finds it intolerable if I make a phone call without paying attention to her. Hissing and spitting, she tries to knock over the telephone. She is clever enough to see the connection between my seemingly senseless talking into a void and the instrument my hand protects. She is indignant. She plants herself before me and pleads for my attention, while my voice addresses someone who obviously does not exist.

People who mean well but who do not understand cats prefer to spend their leisure time listening to the radio or watching television, drinking, smoking, and noisily conversing with their friends. They have little patience for cats and consign them to that nether world of neglected domestic animals. The tie between man and cat is thus broken. It is a sad moment. The cat withdraws into itself in a way that fits its personality. Henceforth, it is about as happy as a deserted woman who pulls herself together and decides never to suffer a broken heart again. For cats do not importune their masters. Instead, they watch them and wait for them, making believe they have more important things to think about. They do not ask for forgiveness because they have good manners and because our human code of honor has nothing to do with theirs. The only exceptions are the Siamese. If they cannot capture one's attention with their big blue eyes, they come right up close and ask, dissatisfaction plainly written on their features, what the individual has against them.

Since cats move about the house with such dignified aloofness, the deliberate and unabashed way in which they suddenly turn on their charm makes cat lovers even more enthusiastic about them than if they always behaved in a proper fashion. In this they resemble a queen who can never be vulgar and yet is capable at any moment of doing shocking things. For instance, an adorable cat may be sitting on her master's shoulder next to his warm neck, apparently lost in dreams. All of a sudden, she breaks out of this reverie: she reaches out a paw for a piece of food on the master's fork and deftly snatches it away. Very rude, isn't it? Yet this is not a case of theft. Didn't the bit of food move on the shiny point of the fork? Well, anything that moves is fair game for a cat. The master bristles and yells: "What got into you?" He shoves the cat from his shoulder. But why is he so incensed? Does he want to chain his cat to him to be spared her sudden whims? He should be delighted at these few amusing acts of mischief on the part of a creature that has mastered self-discipline.

Since cats have humor, quick-wittedness, and imagination, their earliest games are really training exercises to perfect those gifts. Every autumn leaf in the wind represents a mouse or a bird. The histrionic cat does not really believe this about the leaf but plays schizophrenic, mingling reality and fiction. The cat plays this part with concentrated seriousness – and then, when the pantomine is over, dances in wild abandon.

One of the many widespread fallacies about cats is that older cats no longer play and only want to rest. The reason that older ones often stop playing is a shattering indictment of their masters. "Who can say," writes Nabokov in *Lolita*, "how often we break a dog's heart when we stop playing with him?" Cats play a little while longer, all by themselves; but their hearts break, too, perhaps more often than dogs'.

Cats like to play with people, but the latter are often not very imaginative. The usual game is to let a ball of yarn roll under the furniture and have the cat retrieve it. But try playing a game of hide-and-seek with your kitten. As you move quickly you exercise your back and stomach muscles, and you sharpen your sense of sight and touch. The best way to get slow-moving people to move briskly in a circle is to have them dangle a tiny piece of string in front of a cat as the cat darts and leaps at it with its paws. Keeping your cat in a good and playful mood, even when it gets old, and at the same time keeping yourself in trim is invigorating fun.

Sometimes my Siamese cat, Sirikit, lies rolled up in a ball in an armchair. She seems unaware of me as I approach her on tiptoe. But a faint growl in her throat indicates that there is no such thing as an oblivious cat. However, she is polite; she goes on sleeping so as not to spoil the fun I have in surprising her. As she waits with ears and muscles tensed and her throat protests in mild annoyance, my open hand is poised above the armchair. When she was a kitten, she reacted to this vulturelike hand above her with body tremors, tiny ears pressed back, tail quivering, and throat snarling (with occasionally a loud and piteous meow). She would brace herself to endure the agony. Try as she might, she found no remedy for the menacing hand that invariably swooped down on her from on high, accompanied by a sudden outburst of fiendishly human laughter. Nothing could ward off the monstrous hand – neither flight, nor hissing, nor a quick upward thrust of a paw. As soon as the hand made contact, she would utter a plaintive meow, pretend she was frightened, and cozily surrender. Today, Sirikit is more than seven years old, but pretending to be afraid of the pouncing vulture is still one of her favorite games. The tension is still there. She shudders and complains to the armchair of her terrible fate. As soon as the vulture, provoked by the rattle in her throat, grabs hold of her, she pretends to be in mortal terror. Then, right in the midst of this agony, she purrs for sheer delight. To her, this is an Alfred Hitchcock and a Western movie in one. Often, when I don't feel like playing the vulture game, she sends appealing little sounds over my newspaper. Once you have taken a cat to your heart, it behaves like a small child as long as it lives.

Of course, scenes like the one described above are not the only games humans and cats mutually enjoy. Since Siamese cats cannot stop gazing at their masters and are interested in everything that concerns the latter, my little Siamese sometimes looks at me in an ornate silver-edged mirror hanging over my radio set.

In the individualist kingdom of cats there are mirror-blind and mirror-fascinated felines. When someone tells you a story of a cat so hygienic he uses a toilet bowl and even pulls the chain, as a cat fancier you are happy if you can match it with a story of your mirror-cat or your cat who is friendly with dogs. My Sirikit not only recognizes me in the mirror; sometimes she suddenly glances back and compares the man sitting behind her with the image in the glass. She pays no attention to her own mirror image. But when I grimace or clench my fist behind her back, she glares at the insolent person in the mirror and looks around to see how much I was personally involved in that nonsense. If I look innocent, she challenges the person in the mirror to do it again and, with a quick turn of the head, tries to catch me in the act. This mirror game has become a collusive thing between us. So is her chief source of amusement: throwing herself on the stair-carpet and hysterically pretending she has just been brutally trampled on. She repeats this game from step to step, just as she never misses a chance in front of the looking-glass to provoke me into playing. She keeps up a series of insistent meows because I remain engrossed in my book and refuse to play with her. As soon as I turn a page, she brings her dark little head smartly around, just to see whether that stupid creature sitting in the armchair has not also turned a page. If she catches me red-handed, she springs from the radio on to the table, spreads herself in front of me, and assails me with her scorn, annoyance, and triumph. The only way to calm her down is by a heavy dose of flattery. But after a while, even flattery and outbursts of admiration fail to amuse cats. They are more thrilled by fencers who challenge their swiftly pouncing paws; and they never tire of inviting them to brief skirmishes.

Anyone who has grown up with cats has picked up some of their flights of fancy along the way. Only by constantly inventing things can he hope to get to the bottom of what makes a brooding cat tick. Countless cat diaries, from E. T. A. Hoffmann's *Kater Murr* to Gallico's *My Friend Jenny* and Robert Crottet's *Negri*, have strewn these cat ideas over the world.

You have to live for decades among cats to be able to track down a specific cat psychosis that only cats can share. It is a private matter. Cat fanciers live with a nightmare. They secretly fear a catastrophe which they can neither describe nor evoke in their conscious mind. The catastrophe is this: because of their ignorance of cats' ways or their rude behavior toward cats, they will suddenly find themselves washed up in the cat world. Personally, I cannot conceive of a more devastating social upheaval.

So, it is possible that when cat lovers bend over every cat they meet and plead in tones of passionate despair: "Here, kitty, here pussy..." they do so with a purpose. Perhaps they're only testing – frantically testing – to see whether they still have the same secret standing in cat society.

14

Photographer Photograph

4

14

27

45

58

59